D1391113

LAGOON
BOOKS

Puzzle Compilation: Jenny Lynch
Design & Illustration: Linley Clode
Cover Design: James Davies
Editors: Nick Hoare and Simon Melhuish

Published by:
LAGOON BOOKS
PO BOX 311, KT2 5QW, U.K.
CE Keep address for future reference

ISBN 1 89971 205 4

MIND-BENDING

CLASSIC WORD

PUZZLES

All the Mind-Bending Puzzle books have been carefully compiled to give the reader a refreshingly wide range of challenges, some requiring only a small leap of perception, others deep and detailed thought. All four books share an eye-catching and distinctive visual style that presents each problem in an appealing and intriguing way. Do not, however, be deceived; what is easy on the eye is not necessarily easy on the mind!

1. WORD CIRCLES

Form a word from the letters of each circle.

2. PALINDROMES PALACE

A palindrome is a word which reads exactly the same backwards, such as "level" and "refer". Solve the following clues to find more one-word palindromes.

1 Midday

2 Made God-like

3 A musical note

4 A female sheep

5 To look at furtively

6 To consult another authority

3. CITIES

The names of six cities can be found in the diagram above. The letters have been mixed up, but remain in the order in which they occur in the city names. Can you find them?

4. Each of these clues will give you a four letter word, which begins in the square indicated by the arrow. The answer can go round the grid in either a clockwise or anti-clockwise direction.

1 John Paul II
2 ajar
3 to tear or yield
4 mature
5 type of wood

6 landlord's money
7 fruit skin
8 IX
9 tidy

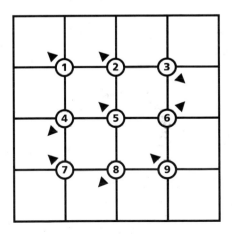

5. TRANSFORMATIONS

Known as Transformations or Doublets, this is a word game which was invented by Lewis Carrol and first published in Vanity Fair in 1879. Players start with two words with the same number of letters and must transform one word into the other, by changing one letter at a time, each time forming a new word. Thus CAT could be changed into DOG like so:

CAT COT DOT DOG.

This was done in three stages. There is more than one way to transform these words but your aim should always be to achieve it in the least possible number of stages. Try the following transformations in six stages:

POOR   APE   MINE

RICH   MAN   COAL

1 MRH STL SSS PD

2 STT CHN TMS VSN N

3 NTH RBR RWR NRL NDR B

4 THR LYB RDC TCH STH WRM

5 THP NSM GTH RTH NTH SWR D

6 BRD NTH HND SWR THT WNT HBS H

6. WORDS OF WISDOM

These popular sayings have been written down without
their vowels and divided into three letter segments. Can
you supply the vowels and word breaks to decipher
the messages?

	A	B	C	D	E
1	O	R	N	T	O
2	A	M	K	A	L
3	E	P	C	E	I
4	S	T	B	R	Y
5	D	U	I	G	N

B1 D4 A1 E3 D4 D3 A4 C4 C5 E5 A3 D1 D3 E1 E4

B3 A2 B4 C3 A1 A2 D2 B4 A3 C1 D2 B3 E3 D4 E5

7. Using the co-ordinates given, choose one of the two letters from the grid and place it in the box below. The correct letters will form a fifteen letter word.

8. Start at the letter R in the centre of the diagram. Move from square to adjoining square and try to form the word RIOT. How many different ways are there of doing this?

			O			
		O	I	I		
	T	T	T	T	O	
O	I	O	R	I	T	T
	I	O	I	O	T	
		I	O	T		
			T			

9. POETRY PLEASE

These poems describe certain cities. In each case, the first letter of each new line spells out which city it is: Try making up your own about: PARIS, MILAN and SYDNEY.

Neon Lights

Everybody's busy

Walk don't walk

Your heart's a flutter

On the subway

Roaring traffic

Keep your wits about you

Very romantic

Enigmatic women

Nocturnal flits

In gondolas

City of dreams

Everlasting

| places |

| plants |

| colours |

| food |

| girl's names |

| occupations |

FRANCE

10. CATEGORIES

The word FRANCE is your keyword. Use each letter of the keyword in turn and try and think up examples of each category. In the first category (place names) examples would be: FENS, RUSSIA, AMSTERDAM, NETHERLANDS, COLOMBIA, ENGLAND.

For example,

– – – – – – butter	**P**	eanut
– – – – – – bunny	**E**	aster
– – – – surplus	**A**	rmy
– – – – – floss	**C**	andy
mad – – – – – –	**H**	atter

Clue: a fruit

11. FILL IN THE BLANKS

The following series of clues (either something-blank or blank-something) will suggest a number of words to you. If you choose the right word each time, the initial letters will spell out another word. The number of dashes will tell you the number of letters in the missing word. All the following will give you words connected with clothing:

1 close - - - - -

     sky - - - -

     soft - - - - - -

     - - - strain

2 - - - - - top

     roll - - - -

     - - - - - fingered

     tea - - - -

     - - - - - shower

     ring - - - -

3 over - - - -

     - - - - - wear

     fist - - - - -

     - - - - - prize

     - - - - out

     space - - - - - - - -

     stinging - - - - - -

     - - - - start

12. WORD SQUARES

A word square is a grid of letters which spell out the same words reading both horizontally and vertically. The clues should enable you to construct a five letter and a four letter word square. A simple one would be:

1. not woman 2. consumed
3. used to catch with

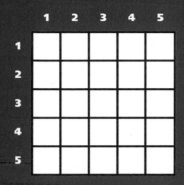

1. part of a wave 2. grasp for 3. keen
4. division within a play 5. trinity

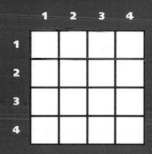

1. examine 2. always 3. partly 4. fall over

SPA ( ) COY

AMP ( ) ASH

WAS ( ) STY

WAX ( ) ABLE

TAP ( ) ODE

MAN ( ) RATE

FIR ( ) ONE

PET ( ) LOW

SPA ( ) SET

13. Find the correct two letters which, when added to the end of the word on the left and the beginning of the word on the right will form two new words. E.G. BRA(SH)APE. The letters you choose should form new words down the centre.

14. If you pair together the correct segments of this circle, you can form sixteen six letter words. What are they?

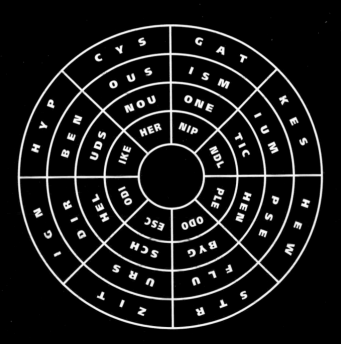

15. Every horizontal and vertical line in the grid contains the consonants of a word, but not necessarily in the correct order. Each word can be completed by the addition of E vowels. There is a two digit number at the end of each line, the first digit tells you the number of consonants in the word, and the second digit, the number of E vowels. All the letters have to be used and each letter is only used once.

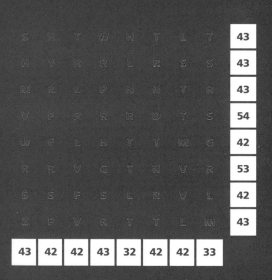

S	R	T	W	H	T	L	T	**43**
H	Y	R	R	L	N	S	S	**43**
M	R	L	P	N	N	T	R	**43**
V	P	R	R	R	D	T	S	**54**
W	F	L	N	T	T	M	G	**42**
R	R	V	G	T	N	V	R	**53**
S	S	F	S	L	R	V	L	**42**
Z	P	V	R	T	T	L	M	**43**

| **43** | **42** | **42** | **43** | **32** | **42** | **42** | **33** |

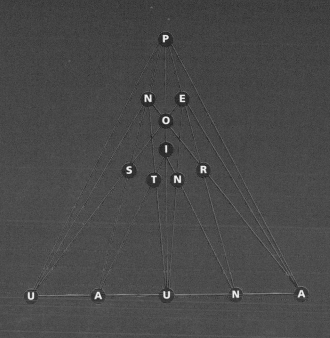

16. Trace along the connecting lines to find a fourteen letter word. You must determine the starting point and you cannot pass through any letter twice.

17. WORD CIRCLES

18. APPLES

How many good apples can you find in the heap below?

```
E  L  E  A  P  P  E  L  A  P  P  L
L  P  P  A  P  L  E  A  P  P  E  A
P  P  L  E  A  L  E  E  P  L  A  E
E  A  P  E  L  L  P  A  P  E  L  P
A  P  P  L  P  P  A  P  L  E  L  P
E  A  L  P  P  E  A  L  E  P  P  A
P  P  E  A  A  P  P  E  L  E  A  L
L  P  P  A  L  A  P  L  E  P  P  E
E  L  A  P  P  P  L  E  P  P  A  L
A  P  L  E  P  P  A  L  L  E  P  P
P  P  E  L  A  P  L  E  E  P  A  A
L  E  A  L  E  L  P  P  A  A  E  P
```

19. LETTER-IN-THE-MIDDLE

If you place the correct letter in the middle of these diagrams, four five letter words can be rearranged from each straight line of letters. Can you find the letter and the words?

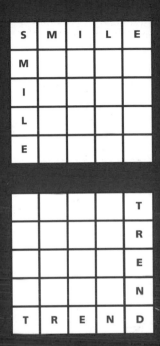

20. WORD SQUARES

Complete the above word squares. The completed square should read the same both horizontally and vertically.

1 Let us un-knot the rope, all together. (6)

2 I felt peaceful until you made me nervous. (7)

3 A special gift is a hidden one. (6)

4 Gifts of these reptiles killed Cleopatra and her cheekiness. (three words, 8 letters)

5 Artists are in the food cupboards, what is relevant? (three words, 8 letters)

6 It is a warning that something is changing. A vital geometric shape which is connecting to someone or something. (five words, 8 letters)

21. ANAGRAMS

The following clues will give you a series of words, which are anagrams of each other. The number in brackets gives you the number of letters in the words. e.g. This church instrument sounds like a cry of pain (5) ORGAN;GROAN

22. HOMOPHONES

The following clues will give you two words which sound alike but are spelt quite differently: e.g. FOWL and FOUL.

1 completely • sacred

2 a place • one of the five senses

3 an agreement • ready to go

4 frill • uneven

5 gangway • surrounded by water

6 amphibian • pulled along

7 a step • look

8 tree • animal covering

9 a fruit • cover with earth

10 army rank • part of a nut

23. LEFT AND RIGHT CHANGE

Change the second letter of each word to the left and the right to form two different words. Put the letter used in the middle. When this has been completed correctly, another word can be read downwards. For example:

SNOG	M	ARID
BIKE	A	RICE
SHIP	N	SLUG

EVES		SNAG
CREW		TREE
RUDE		LANK
TEAR		ARKS
ONUS		SCAR
BOAT		VARY
CLAM		ELOG

24. COMPOSERS

The names of five composers can be found in this diagram. The letters have been mixed up, but remain in the order in which they occur in the original word. Starting from the white S, can you find them all?

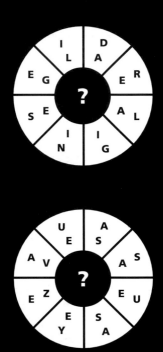

25. WORD-IN-THE-MIDDLE

26. WORDSEARCH

Twenty-one vowelless words are concealed in the letters below. How many can you find?

```
L   Y   M   P   H   Y   S   T   N
Y   H   Y   L   K   H   Y   R   P
S   S   H   Y   L   Y   C   R   Y
P   Y   Y   L   L   B   R   D   H
Y   Y   P   S   T   R   Y   S   T
G   L   Y   M   G   Y   P   Y   P
N   F   R   Y   F   Y   T   L   Y
P   W   Y   R   F   N   B   R   L
L   P   H   R   Y   Y   P   N   Y
F   Y   D   H   C   N   Y   L   R
M   Y   N   R   L   Y   F   N   D
B   M   Y   X   G   S   Y   P   Y
```

27. Complete the following difficult word squares. The completed square should read exactly the same, reading both across and downwards. Clues are given for each word but in no particular order.

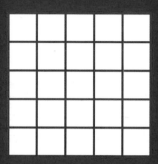

The legitimate existence before a watershed
Dressed up (retro) — a plume

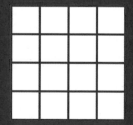

a poison (anagram of a flirty) heard as red light
a prefix meaning blue

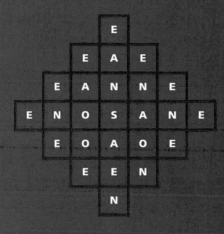

28. Starting at the letter S in the centre, move from square to adjacent square and see how many different ways the word SANE can be formed.

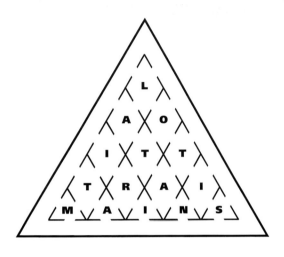

29. Spell out a fifteen letter word by travelling round the triangle, one "room" at a time. You can only go through each room once, but you can use the outside passage as often as you wish.

30. The following clues will give you two words which are anagrams of each other. The number in brackets tells you the number of letters.

1 most severe • beats (8)

2 making whole • adjusting

   one's position (11)

3 conjugally joined • one who likes (7)

4 referee • soiled (6)

5 matures • gunman (6)

6 not smooth • grumble (6)

31. Complete the following word square so that the same four words can be read both across and downwards. Clues are given in no particular order.

- to prevent
- lettuce and tomato
- to get up
- as far as one can go
- words directly to the audience

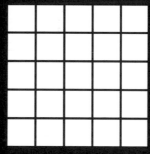

```
A X A O C X E T A L
X M P H O E N I X F
X X E S X N Y R A L
N D X E D N I X T A
A X E P H A R Y N X
L Y F R X E L F Y G
A T H E I J L D S L
H S U F F I X I X M
P A X I N O X U R C
O N Y X C O C C Y X
```

32. How many words, ending with X, can you find in the word square? All words must contain at least three letters.

1	a brood of	a	lions
2	a pride of	b	nightingales
3	a kindle of	c	crows
4	a drove of	d	geese
5	a murder of	e	hens
6	a school of	f	bears
7	a shoal of	g	badgers
8	a sloth of	h	cattle
9	a gaggle of	i	fish
10	a cete of	j	hawks
11	a cast of	k	kittens
12	a watch of	l	bass

33. FARMYARD FRENZY

There are collective nouns used to describe a gathering of certain animals: for example, we talk of a COLONY of ants and a PLAGUE of locusts. Some are more well known than others. Can you match these animals with the correct collective term?

34. MORE CATEGORIES

This time the key word is shorter, but the categories are much more difficult.

PALE

artists

mountains

military leaders

football teams

architecture

fish

35. MORE WORD CIRCLES

STAB		STAR
FLAM		SNAP
PROP		BRED
CROP		MISS
GOAT		SHIP
JOBS		HUNT
ANTS		SPAN

36. Change the second letter of each word to the left and the right, forming two new words. Put the letter used in the middle. When completed correctly, these letters will form a new word down the centre.

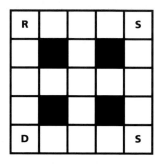

A I R U B I S W C N T E N T E O U

37. Fill in these crosswords using the letters given. There are no clues but you should form six five letter words for each one.

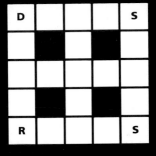

AEITDOPVEIRELRELS

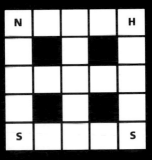

CIOTCIOUDKOENREOT

START HERE

38. You have to find eight words which end with the letter T to fill in the wheel above. Starting with the grid pointing northwards, if you rearrange the scrambled letters to the left of the grid you will discover a new word which is a clue to your missing word ending in T. The number of squares on each grid represents the number of letters in the missing word.

39. The answers to the clues are nine letter words and can be found in the grid below. Each letter can be found in order, on each horizontal line. Every letter is used only once.

1. knitted hood
2. boat
3. savage
4. fraudster
5. to hate

6. comes after deuce
7. like the food of the gods
8. rising
9. madly

B	C	M	A	A	C	B	A	A
M	S	A	H	A	B	A	D	A
R	T	V	L	B	A	N	O	C
R	A	A	R	E	M	A	B	I
N	L	C	O	A	M	I	N	C
K	A	A	S	D	N	T	L	A
A	I	T	A	A	R	I	I	A
V	L	A	A	A	G	T	A	N
L	N	E	Y	A	T	N	N	E

40. Find the word which, when added before the first word and after the second, will give you two new words. E.G. KIND:MILK – the answer would be MAN to give MANKIND and MILKMAN.

1	**2**
MIX	FISH
FAST	BED
LIER	DOCTOR
SHY	GRAM
DON	FORGOT
CROSS	SMITH

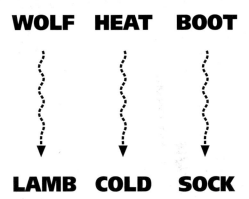

WOLF **HEAT** **BOOT**

LAMB **COLD** **SOCK**

41. Can you change the following words into each other, changing just one letter at a time and always forming a new word at each stage. Change WOLF into LAMB in seven stages, HEAT into COLD in four stages and BOOT to SOCK in four stages.

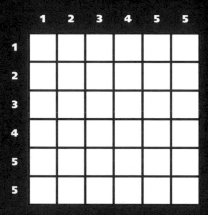

	1	2	3	4	5	5
1						
2						
3						
4						
5						
5						

- not in couples
- choose
- black eye
- help
- rendezvous (plural)
- fireplaces

42. Try this six letter word square. When completed correctly, it should read the same, reading across and downwards. Clues are given in no particular order.

43. Match up the segments from the three triangles and you will form nine words:

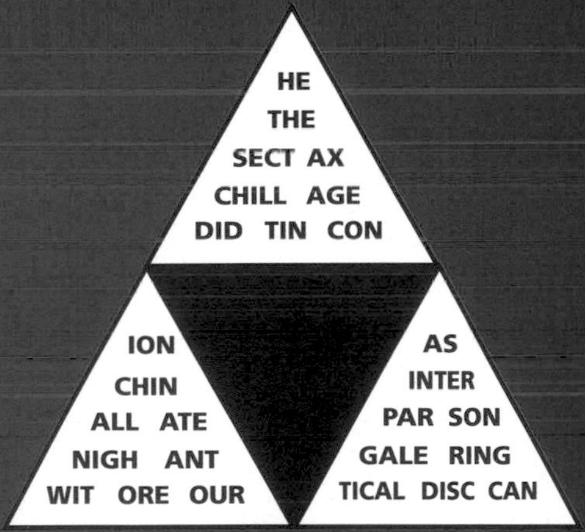

HE
THE
SECT AX
CHILL AGE
DID TIN CON

ION
CHIN
ALL ATE
NIGH ANT
WIT ORE OUR

AS
INTER
PAR SON
GALE RING
TICAL DISC CAN

44. Take away five letters from the following and you will discover a word which is in the Oxford dictionary:

p e g l
f a t i o
o e e t
v i r e l
i s s

N K

K N L

R H S

S H N G N

H G K N T

Y W K S H

R N N G T P

S G S M N

45. The letters above all lack the same vowel to make certain words Once formed, the eight words can be paired up to form four phrases What are they?

R	A	R	N	T	N
T	W	T	R	R	A
N	R	A	A	A	R
A	R	N	W	W	A
W	R	T	W	A	T
A	T	R	A	N	W
N	A	A	R	R	R

46. Divide the letter grid up into six identical shapes so that the word WARRANT can be read six times. No two versions can be alike and the shapes must not overlap.

47. Trace out a thirteen letter word by travelling along the lines. You must not cross a letter twice. You choose the starting letter.

48. Change the first letter of each word to make two new words. Place the new letter in the middle and you should form a new word reading downwards.

TONS		ROTA
WEST		RAVE
PAIN		MINE
DARN		LAST
GAVE		BOLD
HIDE		HELL
AMPS		UNTO
SONG		PAIN
DIMS		BIDE
FAIL		WALK
RATS		ALMS

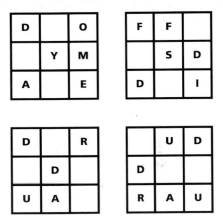

49. Start at a corner square and spiral clockwise to finish at the centre square, spelling out a nine letter word. You have to find the missing letters.

50. Always starting at the top of the pyramid, find seven eight letter words. Each word uses one letter and one letter only from every row, in the correct order of descent. Every letter is used at least once.

51. MORE WORD CIRCLES

52. JUMBLED LETTERS

The following collections of letters can be re-arranged into a phrase or word. The number of brackets tells you the number of letters in each word;

1 AEGIMNNORRSTTTX
It'll blow your socks off (5,6,4)

2 AGGHIIINNNORTWY
Painful to watch (8,2,5)

3 BBEEEEINNNNOOST
A buzzing in your ears? (3,2,4,6)

4 CCCIILMNOORSTUU
Round and round (15)

5 BEEHIIMMRRSSTVY
Ahoy me hearties! (5,2,7)

6 DEEGHLNNOOOSTU
Keep quiet (4,4,6)

7 EEFGILLMNOORSSS
Lovely aroma (8,2,5)

8 EGGIIIINNSSSTWX
Beat generation (8,7)

9 EGIILNNOPPRSSSU
A sign of disapproval (7,4,4)

10 CGIILMNOOPSSSTU
Scandal monger (6,9)

P R / N A	E L / A O	T U / S K	F I / N L	E D / L K
R O / E N		N I / R Y		U T / I N
B S / I A	D I / Q T	E A / D S	B I / E N	R Y / G E
T S / M K		K T / L E		W I / S C
S G / E T	E N / I A	V R / E Y	E T / O K	R T / S K

53. Each square in the crossword contains four letters. You have to find which letter in each square will successfully complete the crossword, forming six words.

54. Change the first letter of each word to the left and right to form two new words. Put the new letter in the middle and you should form a new word reading downwards.

MICE		HIRE
PUMP		NOSE
CAST		VASE
FIRS		KNEW
POST		GILL
STEM		DONS
HARK		FAME
LANK		POUR

55. Trace out a thirteen letter word by following the lines. You must not cross a letter twice and you must choose the starting point.

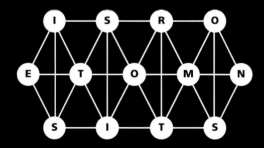

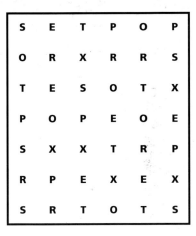

S	E	T	P	O	P
O	R	X	R	R	S
T	E	S	O	T	X
P	O	P	E	O	E
S	X	X	T	R	P
R	P	E	X	E	X
S	R	T	O	T	S

56. Divide the grid up into six identical shapes, each of which contains the same seven letters which can be re-arranged to form a word.

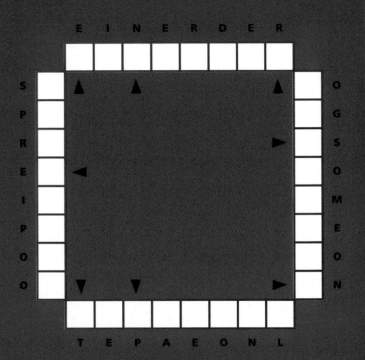

57. Unscramble the four sets of letters to reveal four animals. When these are written in the grid, the arrowed letters can be re-arranged to form another animal.

58. Join the following pairs of letters together to form six six-letter words. One of the pairs is common to all the six words.

AL

AX

PY

MA

BO

WH

SY

SK

ED

AK

AN

IM

CL

59. Find the letter which can be added, in any position, to all three words to form three longer words. When you have found all the letters, these can be read to reveal something edible.

☐ OVERT RAZED MINE	☐ SIRE BAT BOOT

☐ PINT CAT LUNGE	☐ RUSTY REST STAKED

☐ RANGE CARTON HOPED	☐ PAID KIN SIP

 FIN TILED RIDING		RUST SAVE DIN	
TON MOP BAN		RAIN RIVER ROUTE	
FIST BASH FITTER		MAN MEN GROVE	
LUNGE RAM RIM		PARLEY EDGE BAKED	

60. FURTHER TRANSFORMATIONS

Can you change the following words into each other, changing just one letter at a time, and always forming a new word at each stage. Turn NOSE into CHIN in six stages. Turn WITCH into FAIRY in fourteen stages. Turn TEARS into SMILE in six stages.

NOSE WITCH TEARS

CHIN FAIRY SMILE

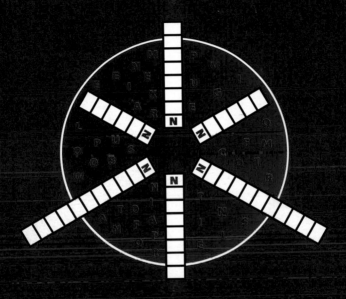

START HERE

61. You have to find six words which end with the letter N to fill in the wheel above. Starting with the grid pointing northwards, if you rearrange the scrambled letters to the left of the grid you will discover a new word which is a clue to your missing word ending in N. The number of squares on each grid represents the number of letters in the missing word.

AACCEENPSSTT

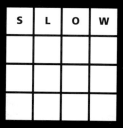

62. Can you arrange the letters in the square so that four words can be read across and four different words can be read downwards? The first line has been done for you.

63. Spell out a fifteen letter word by going round the triangle one "room" at a time. You can go into each room once, but you may use the outside passage as often as you wish.

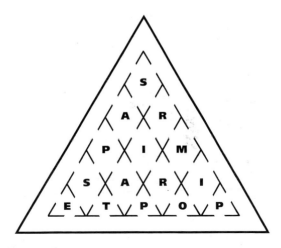

61. MORE WORD CIRCLES

65. The following clues will give you two words which differ only by the inclusion of an extra letter. E.g. hit/yob would give the words clout and lout.

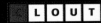

The shaded box in each answer should correspond to this extra letter. When you have answered all the clues, rearrange the letters in the shaded boxes to form a new phrase.

high-flier • story-line
sprightly • infiltrator
started • pulses
to regiment • a herb
carouse • a list
race course • pin
ethical • spoken
quiet • speed
a spice • top card
gather • highland valley
painful sound • female relative

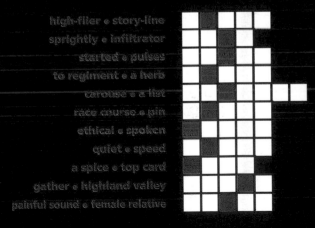

U	T	T	U	E	S
A	E	T	A	R	Y
S	Y	Y	E	Y	S
E	R	S	A	R	A
U	S	U	R	U	E
T	R	T	S	U	T
A	Y	E	A	R	Y

66. Divide the letter grid up to form six identical shapes so that the same seven letter can be formed from the letters in each shape. No two versions can be alike and they do not overlap.

67. Unscramble the following sets of fifteen letters to form phrases. The number in brackets gives you the number of letters in each word and there is a clue for each phrase.

1   A D D E E H L M N N N O O O T
    Neil Armstrong did it (6,2,3,4)

2   A D E G H I L M M N O O R S T
    Making a stormy exit (8,3,4)

3   D E F G J L L L L O O O O W Y
    Birthday boy (5,4,6)

4   D E G G I I I K N N N P R U V
    On the wagon (5,2,8)

5   E E F G H I L N O O P S T T U
    Freudian mistake (4,2,3,6)

6   A C D G H I I N O P P R S T T
    Being clumsy at needlework (8,1,6)

CAVE		SONG
ODDS		ICES
PACK		RUST
DOCK		PEST
BARS		MARL
MACE		BUST
HARD		FELL

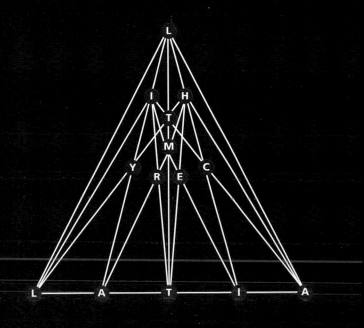

69. Start anywhere and travel along the connecting lines in a continuous path to spell out a 14 letter word. Each circle must only be visited once.

LION   **BANKS**   **CART**

PUMA   **RIVER**   **PONY**

70. Change the following words into each other, changing one letter at a time and always forming a new word at each stage: Change LION into PUMA in six stages. Change BANKS into RIVER in seven stages. Change CART into PONY in six stages.

71. Every horizontal and vertical line in the grid contains the consonants of a word, but not necessarily in the correct order. All the words can be completed by adding O vowels. There is a two figure number at the end of each line; the first digit tells you the number of consonants in the word, the second digit, the number of O vowels. Find the words! All the letters must be used and each letter is used only once.

R	W	S	S	Y	T	T	L	**42**
T	G	Y	R	P	B	T	T	**42**
F	S	F	N	G	H	S	Y	**32**
M	R	W	T	T	K	L	P	**52**
W	L	L	N	S	S	S	V	**22**
P	R	L	T	L	T	R	V	**52**
R	P	S	N	T	S	L	S	**42**
R	R	T	P	T	S	R	T	**22**

53	**42**	**51**	**43**	**51**	**32**	**61**	**32**

72. Divide the grid up into four equal parts, each of which should be the same shape and contain the same 9 letters which can be arranged into a nine letter word.

I	A	S	N	E	L
E	S	G	R	M	N
A	R	I	A	E	S
N	L	R	A	N	L
M	L	G	S	I	G
E	G	M	I	R	M

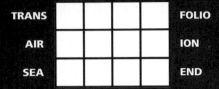

TRANS					FOLIO
AIR					ION
SEA					END

BAT				SELF
ARC				RING
RAI				ON

73. Which three or four letter words, when added to the end of the words on the left and the beginning of the words on the right will form six new words?

PORT   **DROP**   **STAGE**

SHIP   **FALL**   **PLAYS**

74. Can you change the following words into each other, changing one letter at a time, and forming new words at each stage? Change PORT into SHIP in five stages, DROP into FALL in six stages and STAGE into PLAY in five stages.

75. Change the first letter of each word to the left and right to form two new words. Place the new letter in the middle and you should form another new word, reading downwards.

CHIN		PAGE
SKIN		BIDS
DAME		BEAR
ITCH		VAST
SIRE		FILL
BOWL		FOLK

76. CRACK THE CODE

Each letter of the alphabet has been substituted by another to make this cryptogram. Can you decipher it?

IRU HDFK

OHWWHU

XVH WKH

OHWWHU

WKUHH

SODFHV

WR WKH

ULJKW

LQ WKH

DOSKDEHW

Find five musical instruments

```
T  E  O  A  G
U  V  I  L  U
L  R  A  T  I
F  O  E  O  N
B  O  P  I  A
```

Find five drinks

```
D  E  H  C  A
I  R  I  E  L
C  Y  A  T  I
R  R  N  U  O
E  H  S  O  Z
```

77. HIDDEN WORDS

Words have been hidden in the following word squares. To find out what they are, choose a letter to start at and then move from one letter to the next, you can move one up, down, right, left or diagonally. Each letter must only be used once however and all 25 letters must be used.

1 Word Circles:
DESICCATED, GARGANTUAN

2 Palindrome Palace:

1. NOON 2. DEIFIED
3. MINIM 4. EWE
5. PEEP 6. REFER

3 Caracas Cardiff Chicago
Cologne Cordoba
Cairo

4

5

POOR	APE	MINE
BOOR	ARE	MINT
BOOK	ERE	MIST
ROOK	ERR	MOST
ROCK	EAR	MOAT
RICK	MAR	COAT
RICH	MAN	COAL

6 Words of Wisdom:
1 More haste less speed
2 A stitch in time saves nine
3 Neither a borrower nor a
lender be
4 The early bird catches
the worm
5 The pen is mightier than
the sword
6 A bird in the hand is worth
two in the bush

7 PROCRASTINATION

8 Eleven ways

10 Categories

Possible solutions include:

Freesia **R**ose **A**spidistra
Nasturium **C**onifer
Eglantine **F**awn **R**ed **A**zure
Navy **C**erise **E**cru
Frankfurter **R**ice **A**pple
Nougat **C**hocolate **E**ggs
Frances **R**oberta **A**ngela
Nancy **C**lare **E**lizabeth
Farmer **R**ector **A**rtist
Newsagent **C**hef **E**mbalmer.

11 Fill In The Blanks:

SHAVE	CLIFF	COAT
HIGH	**O**VER	**U**NDER
OPTION	LIGHT	FIGHT
EYE	LEAF	FIRST
	APRIL	LOOK
	ROAD	**I**NVADERS
		NETTLE
		KICK

12 Word Squares:

```
C R E S T     T E S T
R E A C H     E V E R
E A G E R     S E M I
S C E N E     T R I P
T H R E E
```

13 DELETE, ENERGY, STALIN

14
odours	eschew	benign
zither	nipple	helium
schism	pseuds	dirndl
cystic	bygone	odious
strike	nougat	hyphen
flukes		

15 1 – 8 equals horizontal, and A – H equals vertical words.

1 ESTHETE	**A** WHEEZES
2 EYELESS	**B** PREFER
3 ELEMENT	**C** FERRET
4 PERSEVERE	**D** SWEEPER
5 HELMET	**E** TEETH
6 REVENGER	**F** RENTED
7 SELLER	**G** VELVET
8 LEVERET	**H** EMERGE

16 SUPERANNUATION

17 Word Circles:
MIGRAINE, HYSTERICAL

18 Apple Search:
there are only two

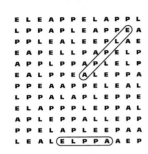

19 Word-In-The-Middle
1 **P** (ripen, ramps, plant, tulip)
2 **T** (tapes, asset ,terms ,afoot)

20 Word Squares:

```
S M I L E     Y E A S T
M A N I A     E A G E R
I N S E T     A G A V E
L I E G E     S E V E N
E A T E R     T R E N D
```

21 Anagrams:

1 untied / united
2 restful / fluster
3 talent / latent
4 presents / serpents / pertness
5 painters / pantries / pertains
6 alerting / altering / integral / triangle / relating

22 Homophones:
wholly / holy   site / sight
pact / packed   ruff / rough

aisle / isle   toad / towed
stair / stare   fir / fur
berry / bury   colonel / kernel

23 WHISPER

24 Stravinsky   Satie   Schumann
Schubert   Strauss

25 More Word-In-The-Middle
1 **V** (divan, gavel, verse, vigil)
2 **M** (seamy, mazes,
mauve, amuse)

26 Wordsearch

pygmy	tryst	crypt	shyly
lymph	lynch	myrrh	gypsy
lynx	thy	try	cry
dry	fly	fry	spy
sly	shy	ply	my
pry			

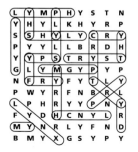

27 Word Squares

```
TANGO    STOP
ALIEN    TAME
NINES    OMEN
GEESE    PENT
ONSET
```

28 21 ways

29 TOTALITARIANISM

30 1. harshest   thrashes
     2. integration orientating
     3. married   admirer
     4. umpire   impure
     5. ripens   sniper
     6. rugged   grudge

31 Word Squares:

```
SALAD
ARISE
LIMIT
ASIDE
DETER
```

32

coax	pax	latex	crux
onyx	six	coccyx	index
phoenix	sex	styx	flax
phalanx	axe	apex	prefix
pharynx	flex	cox	suffix
syntax			

33 Farmyard Frenzy:

1e	2a
3k	4h
5c	6i
7l	8f
9d	10g
11j	12b

34 More Categories

Possible solutions include

Picasso Angelico Leonardo
daVinci El Greco
Pyrenees Andes
Lammermuirs, Etna
Paton Attila Leonidas
Eisenhower
Preston Arsenal Leeds Utd,
Everton
Pergola Alcove Lobby Eaves
Pike Angelfish Lobster Eel

35 Word Circles:
MELODIOUS, RHYTHMIC

36 COLONIC

37 Cross Words

```
R E S T S
A   C   I
B R O W N
I   N   U
D U E T S
```

```
D R E S S   N O T C H
I   L   T   O   O   U
V I O L A   D I N E R
E   P   R   E   I   T
R E E D S   S O C K S
```

38 The clue is in brackets.

ITINERANT	(traveller)
COBALT	(element)
TOURNAMENT	(competition)
CAVEAT	(warning)
PERTINENT	(relevant)
AFFECT	(pretend)
DISCONTENT	(unease)
MISSPENT	(wasted)

39 1. BALACLAVA
2. CATAMARAN
3. BARBARIAN
4. CHARLATAN
5. ABOMINATE

6. ADVANTAGE
7. AMBROSIAL
8. ASCENDANT
9. MANICALLY

40 CAKE
STEAD
ATE
MAR
TEN
WORD

41 WOLF   HEAT   BOOT
WOLD   HEAD   BOOK
SOLD   HELD   COOK
SOLE   HOLD   COCK
SOME   COLD   SOCK
SAME
LAME
LAMB

42 Word Square

A S S I S T
S H I N E R
S I N G L Y
I N G L E S
S E L E C T
T R Y S T S

43 withering   theoretical
intersection   consonant
chinchillas   discourage
candidate   nightingale
parallax

44 Literally take away "five letters"from

AFPIOVELLOEGTTIERESS
......and you get **APOLOGIES**

45 shining knight
missing link
printing ink
Irish whisky

46

R	A	R	N	T	N
T	W	T	R	R	A
N	R	A	A	A	R
A	R	N	W	W	A
W	R	T	W	A	T
A	T	R	A	N	W
N	A	A	R	R	R

47 GALVANISATION

48 INVESTIGATE

49 1. dromedary
2. daffodils
3. laundered
4. mudguards

50 coercion

conceive
concerts
concords
choleric
cheroots
chortles

51 Word Circles:
GUARANTEED, CYCLICALLY

52 Jumbled words

1 Extra strong mint
2 Writhing in agony
3 Bee in one's bonnet
4 Circumlocutions
5 Shiver my timbers
6 Hold one's tongue
7 Smelling of roses
8 Swinging sixties
9 Pursing one's lips
10 Gossip columnist

53 Crossword

R O U N D
O   N   U
A D D E R
S   E   S
T A R O T

54 The word is DREAMILY

55 MONSTROSITIES

56 The word is EXPORTS

S	E	T	P	O	P
O	R	X	R	R	S
T	E	S	O	T	X
P	O	P	E	O	E
S	X	X	T	R	P
R	P	E	X	E	X
S	R	T	O	T	S

57 REINDEER   MONGOOSE
ANTELOPE   PORPOISE

The arrowed letters form the
word TERRAPIN.

58 MAIMED WHIMSY SKIMPY
AKIMBO ANIMAL CLIMAX

59 CHOCOLATE DROPS

60 NOSE   WITCH   TEARS
NOTE   WINCH   SEARS
COTE   WENCH   STARS
CORE   TENCH   STARE
CORN   TENTH   STALE
COIN   TENTS   STILE
CHIN   TINTS   SMILE
        TILTS
        TILLS

FILLS
FALLS
FAILS
FAIRS
FAIRY

61 REVISION (re-examine)

RESIGN (give up)

CONSOLATION (comfort)

TACITURN (silent)

DESECRATION (profanation)

TUREEN (soup bowl)

62 S L O W
C A P E
A C T S
N E S T

63 MISAPPROPRIATES

64 Word Circles:
PALATABLE, ASTHMATIC

65 The shaded letters form the words:

MIRROR IMAGE

PILOT PLOT
SPRY SPY
BEGAN BEAN
DRILL DILL
ROISTER ROSTER

TRACK TACK
MORAL ORAL
PEACE PACE
MACE ACE
GLEAN GLEN
GROAN GRAN

66 The word is ESTUARY

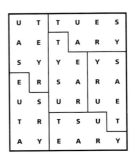

U	T		T	U	E	S
A	E		T	A	R	Y
S	Y		Y	E	Y	S
E	R		S	A	R	A
U	S		U	R	U	E
T	R		T	S	U	T
A	Y		E	A	R	Y

67 1 Landed on the moon

2 Slamming the door

3 Jolly good fellow

4 Given up drinking

5 Slip of the tongue

6 Dropping a stitch

68 GALLERY

69 ARITHMETICALLY

70 LION BANKS CART
LOON BARKS CARE
LOOP BARES CANE
POOP PARES CONE
POMP PAVES BONE
PUMP RAVES BONY
PUMA RAVER PONY
RIVER

71 **1 – 8** equals horizontal, and
A – H equals vertical words.

1 TORSOS A TOMORROW
2 GROTTO B SORROW
3 GOOFY C SOFTLY
4 WORKTOP D PONTOON
5 SOLO E SPOTTY
6 TROLLOP F BOOTH
7 SPOONS G STROLLS
8 SOOT H VOLVO

72 The word is MALINGERS

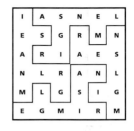

I	A	S	N	E	L
E	S	G	R	M	N
A	R	I	A	E	S
N	L	R	A	N	L
M	L	G	S	I	G
E	G	M	I	R	M

73 HER, PORT

74 PORT DROP STAGE
SORT PROP STARE
SOOT POOP STARS
SHOT POOL STAYS
SHOP POLL SLAYS
SHIP PALL PLAYS
FALL

75 SAFETY

76 **The message is:–** "For each letter use the letter three places
to the right in the alphabet."

77 **Hidden Words:**
flute, viola, guitar, oboe, piano,
ale, chianti, ouzo, sherry, cider